PEARL'S JOURNEY
IN SEARCH OF A HOME

by

Terry Bushey

Illustrated by

Lorna Murphy

I would like to dedicate this book to:

Valerie Lang Waldin HVCC Animal Law Professor and core inspiration who provided me with the tools and knowledge to fight for those who have no voice.

Crazy Paws Dog Rescue Group - Thank you for saving Pearl and all other dogs through rescue, transport, and foster.

Dianne DelPozzo (Aunt Di) and Kim Nantista, the amazing Canine Good citizen and Certified Therapy dog trainers.

Aubree D. Dockal, my sweet granddaughter (little tyke)

Much love and support from my husband Michael Bushey and my daughters Valerie, Kaitlyn and Sara.

My Mom and Dad for the years of growing up with animals.

In memory of my Grandmother June Degener and my Pitbull Luna. Thank you for listening to my prayers.

To all the heroes who can hear the cries of those who cannot speak:
Thank you for all you do!

Hello, my name is Pearl. I think I'm a good dog.

I love being alive, and I enjoy all that life has to offer.

It's a big beautiful world. I love relaxing in the warm sunlight, rolling in the fresh green grass, looking up at the trees, and chasing the bumblebees with the wind in my face blowing my cheeks up so I look silly.

But it wasn't always like this.

Four years ago, I didn't even have a name. I was not allowed to walk around, run, play, or explore. I didn't get fed often for days at a time. I drank mostly from puddles. I didn't have a warm house, soft bed, or loving touch of a caring human hand. The angry humans did not care that I was a living breathing soul that could feel pain, suffering, hunger, sadness, or the fact that I needed exercise, good food, water, and love. None of that mattered. My life just didn't matter.

I was so so sad. The humans I lived with seemed

angry and were bullies that didn't treat me well. The only reason I was there was so the humans could make something called money. That was where I came in.

They tried to make me do things I knew were wrong! They wanted me to fight and bully another dog. I learned that other angry people would pay money to watch dogs fight, betting on who wins. I did not want to fight, and neither did the other dogs. I was confused, and I didn't have a human voice so I couldn't defend myself. I knew this was wrong, and I refused to fight.

Once the humans learned I wouldn't fight. I was afraid of what they would do to me. But they had a different plan. They used me for breeding, which means I would have litter after litter of puppies that would be sold. It was hard on my body. I was tired. I missed my puppies. They were taken away too early. I had more to teach them, but the angry and greedy humans were anxious to sell and make their money.

One day out of nowhere. I was unchained from the rusted run-down leaky doghouse and was taken on a car ride. Wow, this was exciting! I stuck my head out of the window, my tongue was flapping around, and I felt the cool air in my face. When the car stopped, I was dropped off on the side of the road.

I heard the angry human say, "She's too old to have puppies, and she isn't making us any money, so she's no longer needed." And just like that I was abandoned.

Alone and scared, but I didn't lose hope. I kept dreaming and thinking about having a forever home.

As I was feeling down and empty, a lady walked slowly toward me. I didn't know what to do. She seemed very gentle and whispered to me, "My poor dear dog, let me get you off the streets. It's dangerous. You could get hit by a car or starve."

She brought me to a place called an animal shelter. She said I would have food, shelter, and a chance to find a home. Oh boy, that was exciting! I was very grateful!

The animal shelter was very loud and crowded, but I did get a good bowl of yummy dog food, and I wasn't lost outside. I heard one of the animal shelter workers say I only had seven days to find a home, and because I was a "pit bull" it would be even harder to find a home because no one adopts them since they are scary looking, mean, and they fight.

I thought, *Was I a pit bull?* I'm not mean, but the angry humans wanted me to be mean and to make me fight. But that's not me. That's not who I am. There were many others like me who did not want to fight, either.

The only ones that did fight only did it to please their humans. But I knew better. I knew fighting was wrong.

On day six of being at the animal shelter, a nice lady from dog rescue group was picking out dogs that needed help. She came to my cage looked into my eyes and said, "I'm getting you out of here, and we are going on a trip to your new foster home."

Yippie! That was happy news since I didn't know what would happen after day seven. Phew!

The nice lady said, "You will be going on a long trip in a big van with other abandoned dogs that need help to a place where you will meet your foster mom who will care for you and try and find you your forever home." I was very excited.

I finally arrived at my foster home along with other rescue dogs, I was nervous and kept to myself. Some dogs were nice, and some were very scared.

We were all confused and wondering what would become of us? Where would we go now? There was a very little dog that came to me with big tearful eyes. She seemed to sense that I was scared too. All she wanted to do was curl up next to me and snuggle. It was nice. She felt warm and loving, so I let her. It was crowded, but I was safe.

I'd never been inside a home before. I'd only dreamed of what it was like. I didn't know what to do or where to do my poos and pees. So, I had a lot of what humans call "accidents". I didn't know what to do with dog toys. I was chewing on things called the carpet and the couch. The human said that was naughty, and I needed to learn manners.

There were these things called stairs you had to climb them to get to another room. They were scary. I felt lost and out of place, but I had food and a soft bed to lay on. I was grateful.

Every Sunday, all the foster dogs and I went to a pet store and waited for a family to come adopt us. A lot of the other dogs found forever homes, and it was great! I was happy for them, and I continued to wait patiently for mine.

Week after week went by and still no family. I think it was because I was still confused on what to do. All the other dogs knew how to sit play fetch, stay, walk on a leash, climb stairs, and play with dog toys. They didn't have accidents like me.

I needed a family to help me learn how to be a dog. Then the name "pit bull" came up again about how they can be hard to find homes for. I didn't understand. I was a nice dog. All I wanted was to love and be loved, even though I was around some angry bad humans. I knew humans were not all bad, just like dogs were not all bad, even the so-called "pit bull" dogs. I never gave up hope. I still waited for my forever home. Months went by, and I watched many dog friends come and go to their forever homes.

One Sunday morning, I went to the pet store as usual

and waited. I was sad that day. I just plopped down and laid there dreaming of having a family and what it would be like. I sighed a few times. All the other dogs were excited, wagging their tails and meeting and greeting people. I closed my eyes. All of a sudden, I felt a very warm gentle hand and a soft voice talk to me. I looked up and saw a very nice couple. The lady sat down next to me, and I slowly felt the need to curl up in her lap. It felt like a golden ray of sunshine just shined down on me. We just sat there for quite a while. I heard her say she knew a lot about pit bull dogs and that they are not all bad and any dog can be mean just like some people can be mean. I just knew this was it. I was going home! And just like that I was adopted and on my way to my forever home.

I was saved.

I said goodbye to my foster family by giving sloppy kisses. I was thankful they took me into their home and kept me safe. I arrived at my new home. I was excited and nervous at the same time. I hoped they would like me. I had a new mom and dad and a new sister named Sandy. She was a German shepherd.

My family was very patient and gentle with me and gave me time to get used to my new home. They petted me softly and showed me where the food bowl and bed were. It was great. I had my very own bowl, soft bed, toys, bones, and a leash and collar. And guess what? There was a name tag on my collar. It said Pearl! I had a name.

My name was Pearl, and my life mattered!

It was time to learn how to be a dog.

My new sister, Sandy, taught me how to be a good watchdog, how to chase birds and squirrels, and how to play fetch with a ball. She also taught me how to relax and sleep upside down without a care in the world. Sandy showed me where to hide when my family says it's bath time along with some other human words and what they meant like walk, car ride, and cookie. They were all good words. It meant something good was about to happen.

Sandy was a great sister.

Learning to climb stairs was scary for me, but with my family's patience and good training, I did it. My mom put a cookie on each step. Every time I stepped up, I got a tasty treat. Sister Sandy would run up and down to show me it was easy, like a piece of cake. In no time, I was climbing the stairs! I also learned if I do my pees and poos outside, I got a tasty treat. When I was chewing the couch, Mom will say *no* and then give me a chew bone instead.

That was how I learned how to be a good dog.

One day a visitor came over. I loved seeing new people, but this was a very little human called a baby. She was part of our family. Her name was Aubree. She reminded me of my long-lost puppies, and I loved her instantly. I protected her like she was my own. If she cried, I would alert my family and stay with her and gently lick her tears away. I also watched out the window to make sure squirrels and birds stay away just like sister Sandy taught me. I would lay by her while she slept, and she would feed me some of her cookies when no one was looking. My mom and dad were so proud of me and how far I'd come learning and growing. They wanted to continue my training.

I was going to dog school.

This was exciting! I was going to school to learn new things. It was hard at first. I practiced every day with my mom to sit, lay down, stay, and heel. I worked very hard, and soon enough I got an award for passing my first class. After that, I went to another class to learn how to be a therapy dog.

This was my favorite class because I was able to be with children and older humans that were just as happy to see me as I was to see them. I was taught my manners like not to jump and to always be calm and gentle and that came easy for me.

At the end of school, I got my therapy dog license and certificate. I was now a certified therapy dog—now doesn't that sound fancy?—and I had a new job! It was fantastic! I visited schools, sat with children in the classroom, and they would read me stories. I was told that children reading to me helped them gain confidence to become better readers and better public speakers as adults, simply because I was a good listener and I never judged. I was just so happy to be with them and listen.

It was the best job in the world.

That's my story. I was so happy I was given a chance to live my life and be the best version of a dog I could ever be. All due to the kind-hearted humans that helped me along the way from the nice lady that saw me in the street, then another kind-hearted soul that took me out of the animal shelter to send me to a foster home, and finally my forever home. I have no voice. I can't call for help. It takes kindhearted people to help dogs just like me. I'm now able to give back by helping children become the best versions of a child they can be. Shower me with kindness and watch me grow.

Hello, my name is Pearl, and my life matters!

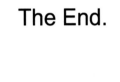

The End.

About the Author

Terry A. Bushey was born and raised in Albany, New York. She is married and mother of three compassionate children. She has a calm nature and a way of bonding with animals, always helping stray dogs or cats and nursing injured wildlife. Because of her gentle nature and soft touch, she always gave animals their space, freedom to be who they are, and they gained her trust quite quickly usually ending up with an inseparable bond.

As an adult, Terry worked at an animal hospital that cared for and nursed the ill, making their lives more comfortable. Terry attended animal law classes to gain knowledge on how to help enforce stricter laws on animal abuse and neglect, as well as worked with rescue groups that organized visits to middle schools to teach humane education to children using pit bull therapy dogs as models.

Over the years, she has learned all animals are individuals with their own unique personalities and should be treated as such. She is a firm believer that animals can talk if you learn how to listen. She also has a love for children hoping to teach them how to listen with their hearts and help animals who can't defend themselves and to notice when an animal is in need and how to help. She rescued a Staffordshire Bull Terrier named Pearl who is an unforgettable inspiration and true role model of the misunderstood breed.

Made in the USA
Middletown, DE
25 August 2020